DIARY OF A MAD IMPERIALIST

With an Essay on the Spirit of the German People

by
Thorsten Pattberg

**lod
press
new
york**

Printed in the United States

Preface

"GERMAN culture is unique, not universal. Certain characteristics explain why Germany became what it became, and did onto others what it had to. Ever since their discovery of China, German missionaries and philosophers had feverishly tried to convert the Chinese to Christianity and the Greco-Hellenic ways. That included a form of brutal 'language imperialism' by which all important Chinese key terminologies were translated into biblical and philosophical words and categories. The result, to this day, is a German 'Chinabild' that is virtually *Chinese-free*." –T Pattberg

THORSTEN PATTBERG

DIARY OF A
MAD IMPERIALIST

We cannot and we must not become Chinese, and at heart we don't want to either. We must not seek ideal or higher meaning of life in China or in any other thing of the past; otherwise we lose ourselves and adhere to a fetish.
--Hermann Hesse, 1921

SHANGHAI, March 2012 - About 111 years ago, the German emperor, Wilhelm II., farewelled the East-Asian Expedition Corps from Bremen's harbor to China in order to crush down on Beijing's resistance movement to European imperialism. His orders were unequivocal: *Bring* civilization to China; *Show* no mercy to reactionaries; and *Teach* China a memorable lesson so that "no Chinaman would ever dare to look askance at one of us." Things of course have changed since then.

Airplanes have been invented. Germany's Federal Minister of Education and Research, Dr. Annette Schavan, and her delegation of top officials once again landed in rainy Shanghai.

China's Pearl River Delta's megalopolis is more populous than Germany's capital, Berlin, and Hamburg, Munich, Cologne, Frankfurt, Stuttgart and the next ten biggest German cities combined. It is gigantic.

The Federal Minister and her decorated entourage certainly preferred the icy north and Beijing, the head of the Chinese *dragon*, over the creature's guts: the damp southern regions of Jiangnan. Yet, although Beijing was the center of China's politics and educational policy, most of the *schaffenden* Germans, all those who actually produce material value since bilateral trade agreements began in 1979, had traditionally settled down in Shanghai or, farther down in the industrial south, in Shenzhen and Guangdong, China's two supreme manufacturing bases. Today, over 5,300 German companies are active in China, and 8,000 German administrators are stationed in Shanghai alone.

The Tongji University of Shanghai is a German partner of choice. It was co-founded by Germans, handed honorary degrees to politicians like Gerhard Schröder, the former

Chancellor, and invites German lecturers by the droves. That said, there are barely 250 German persons studying full-time in all of China; most of them staying no longer than a single academic exchange year or less, and sitting those notorious *dui wai hanyu* classes ("Chinese for foreigners"). Compare those figures to the 25,000 proper Chinese students who study in Germany for real. And, unlike the Chinese in Germany, the Germans in China aren't obliged to provide evidence of 200 hours language work prior to applying for a student visa. The Germans treat Chinese as inferior; and the Chinese treat Germans as superior; that is the way it is; mainly so, perhaps, because both people are carrying themselves in their respective ways for centuries.

Over two dozen German professor chairs at 'Tongji' are currently sponsored by German corporations; most of those senior fellowmen don't speak a word Chinese, of course: Not learning the language of the colonized is an old tradition that I will not explain here. Needless to say, Chinese translators –mostly females- are always cheap and plenty in supply: ten for the price of one German interpreter.

Meanwhile, the German political parties, the German media, the German Academic Exchange Service, the Max-Planck Society, the German Chamber of Commerce, the Goethe Institutes –all state sponsored, pro-government organizations- have arrived in the Middle Kingdom already with the single most important mission to make the Chinese do like the Europeans do, or else to start *chinabashing* the entire place.

Germany's hostility against China is legendary. It is also official: German media constantly demonizes the country because it is too Chinese and too communist. According to the Asia-strategy-paper of October 23rd 2007, the ruling Christian Democratic Union (CDU) and its junior partner the Christian Social Union (CSU) -you thought Germany was a secular place, didn't you?- named China a "threat to European values, and to economic and political developments."

But let us come back to our Federal Minister: At Tongji's 'Chinesisch Deutsches Hochschulkolleg', she gave a prominent lecture that day, or shall we say: she lectured the Chinese, on the sensitivities of "global responsibility." It all amounted rather suspiciously to a Western monologue about how China should do itself after Europe.

Indeed, the Germans try to rectify Chinese culture whenever they can: German officials in Shanghai, illiterate in Chinese language and tradition, complain that Chinese family names and first names are *backwards* (the family name precedes the given name) and thus should be re-arranged in a proper European manner so that manager Wang Yuhe becomes "Yuhe Wang," worker Jin Li becomes "Li Jin," and neighbor Li Hao becomes "Hao Li." Only largely publicized statesmen or dissidents are excluded from this German insult, not at all out of respect or courtesy but mainly because naive German journalists largely follow and imitate US-Anglophone news reporting which, luckily, has yet to produce a single instance of "Zedong Mao," "Weiwei Ai," or "Jinping Xi." For all others of the 1.3 billion Chinese in China, however, they'd better adopt the proper Western ordering of names or else the Germans do it for them.

Germany cannot, for historical reasons, patronize the English-speaking world order (let by the mighty United States), of course, but most smaller European states, the global south, and the developing world, it can and does belittle: Western observers are reminded today of the first Prussian diplomatic mission to East-Asia, the Eulenburg Expedition. In 1861, when Great Britain and France had just invaded Beijing over a commercial dispute concerning opium, Count Friedrich Albrecht zu Eulenburg forced a commercial treaty upon the Qing Empire on behalf of the entire German Customs Union. These days, the Germans consult China on behalf of the entire European Union: "We Europeans," they kick off most Sino-German bilateral negotiations, appearing bigger and more important than they are.

Now, are China's and Germany's research industries compatible? Of course they are –if the Chinese become more German. *No other future scenario exists.* The idea that Germany could learn *anything* from China is absurd –the Chinese want to drive German cars –Porsche, Benz, Audi, BMW– just as bad the Germans do. It is the metaphor of the day.

Are China's and Germany's educational systems compatible? The answer is a clear *mafan* (trouble). First, Germany historically lacks elite universities and university rankings which we so naturally find in the United States, the United Kingdom, Japan, or China. You will see direktoren and professoren flown in from such obscure places like Bochum- or Greifswald University who then co-chair with Chinese elite technocrats who graduated from Asia's most competitive schools like Peking-, Tsinghua-, or Fudan University. It's an honor for the Germans, but for the Chinese? They would rather work with their equals from Harvard in the US or Cambridge in the UK. Learning English from Germans can be annoying, too.

Second, numbers matter: Germany comprises just 1.2% of the world's population, China 20%. Germany united in 1871 AD, China in 221 BC. However, since the Germans indulge in the oriental fantasy that Europeans (the quality people) are of greater world-historical significance than Asians (the quantity people), hence they frequently step into embarrassing categorical fallacies: We recently followed the ego of Horst Seehofer, Minister President of Bavaria, a German county with barely the population size of a Chinese city, on his fleeting trip to Beijing, who was left enraged and in disbelief as to why China's then-President, Hu Jintao, and his Premier, Wen Jiabao, felt no obligation to receive this petty and arrogant German man.

Next, the old German education system has worn out –it's now slowly modeled after the Anglo-Saxon one. As long as German degrees back in the 20th century eluded all comparison, the Germans felt big about themselves and assumed intellectual and cultural superiority. Unfortunately, ever since the so-called 'Bologna Reform' finalized in 2010, German students can now be evaluated against their global peers. It turns out that German test scores, according to the 'OECD Programme for International Student Assessment', rank merely in the global middlefield. Ironically, Shanghai students now rank officially as the best students on the planet.

Last, Germany is a class society based on heredity with a three-tier school system that reflects its class consciousness. It essentially means that children, after having spent four years in primary school together, are separated by the age of ten years onto three different school forms. This will then pre-determine a young person's life and career long before he or she understands the importance of grades and higher education, letting alone having reached sexual maturity.

The United Nations believe, rightly so, that the Teutonic education system is rigged in favor of parents, not children, and condemn Germany for it –to little avail. China, on the other hand, practices its Confucian love for learning for more than two millennia, resulting into a class-blind, clear-cut meritocracy that allows all the children of China, in theory, to take part in the nation's college entrance examination –today known as the *Gaokao*. This is all a mystery to German elites, or, maybe, it is their worst nightmare.

Indeed, the German spirit is a peculiar one. Germany never experienced the Enlightenment —only its own inward-looking form of *Aufklärung; it* lacks the crucial development where the Anglo-Saxon world learned and mastered, by experience, to co-exist in diversity and to tolerate cultural pluralism.

To this day, German culture lacks a holistic conception of humanity; it prefers a linear way of thinking with European culture prominently ahead of China and others. Everything non-European is seen as an awkward deviation from German or Western standard. Unsurprisingly, Angela Merkel, the Chancellor, recently reiterated that multiculturalism was dead in Germany. It means that all foreigners, with the exception of US citizens since Germans are fearful of American power and retaliation, must be *assimilated*, not only in Germany, but also abroad. That's why the Germans in Shanghai will always be German, no matter what, and it will be the submissive Chinese who are forced to integrate and adjust.

If we don't talk about it, imperialism never stops. It changes paradigm, then rattles on. A

Chinese student recently asked me: Do the Germans want to teach more Chinese students because they are really interested in us, or just because the Americans were doing it first?

I vaguely recalled our mission and replied dutifully: No, this commitment to teaching orientals we truly share. It is our global responsibility to make you more like us. That's why we are back in China. Yet again.

E N D

Annette Schavan was forced to resign as Germany's Federal Minister of Education some months after her Shanghai trip. Her former university has found over 60 cases of plagiarism in her doctoral thesis, and thus revoked her doctorate degree. She now works as German ambassador for the Catholic cause in Rome, Italy.

THE SPIRIT OF THE GERMAN PEOPLE

BEIJING, July 2014 - After the Great Wars, the United States colonized the German lands and broke their spirit. The Reich was *de-nazified*, but *also de-Germanized*, with the result that German culture, German philosophy, and German sciences all came to an end. Germany was turned into a proper Western nation and learned to know its place.

That this *is* so, and never happened otherwise, few politicians have any illusions about, except during this mid-summer of 2014, when the leaders in Berlin witnessed a nationwide protest against the recent massive American CIA/NSA surveillance operation targeting not only suspicious German politicians, terrorists, and businessmen but also the entire German population –just in case.

And just when the masters of Washington feared that the rebellious Germans could make impossible demands for more sovereignty and cultural autonomy in the future, it soon became clear to observers that the puppet regime in

Berlin, quite to the contrary, always desperately wanted to join the US planetary surveillance operation, on the condition of becoming America's prime associate and right hand of the Anglo-American empire, not just the butt of it.

Anyone who lived in Germany during the last thirty years had to experience firsthand how this nation finalized its transformation into a US satellite state with a tinsel culture. Most branches of German *Geisteswissenschaften* and German *Literatur* are either discontinued, dead, or dying. Its archaic Humboldt'sche education system and those *magisters*, *diplomas*, and *doctorates* ceased to exist; now German universities imitate the Anglo-Saxon-style grading and credit system with its bachelors (BA), masters (MA), and PhD degrees.

Cinemas exclusively run Hollywood movies. The Germans are slaves to US propaganda every waking minute: news services simply copy and translate about 90% of their contents from Anglophone sources. The younger generations watch *Lost*, *Game of Thrones*, *Homeland*, or *Breaking Bad* –US television series. Teenagers play X-Box, adore US celebrities, and Apple computers or iphones. Office workers sip Starbucks coffee, type on Dell or HP laptops, use Microsoft Office software, and –during their lunch breaks– eat at McDonalds, Pizza Hut, or Kentucky Fried Chicken.

Germans are completely dependent on the internet which -let us be realistic and honest- basically consists of US companies dressed as "global" public services such as *Google*, *Yahoo*, *Youtube*, *Facebook*, *Linkedin*, *Twitter*, *Wikipedia*, *Huffington Post*, *Instagram*, *Ebay*, *Amazon* and hundreds more.

German companies, if they are big and smart enough, don't want to have anything to do with the provincial German ways; instead they'd rather present themselves as "international," meaning American -because that's where all the theories come from, including the rules of global business, the financial structures, the monetary regulations, letting alone business ethics, language, and corporate culture.

From an historical point of view Germans are well known to assimilate happily into American culture and apply for US citizenship. About 40 million Americans today are reported to have German ancestors. Yet, no self-respecting American, if he or she fully understands their country's status in the world, would readily volunteer to become a German citizen.

The English language and tens of thousands of loanwords like *news, dating, meeting, deadline, download,* and *abefuckt* have become so dominant in business, politics, entertainment, culture, arts, education, science, and the world wide web, that growing up as a German speaker, in a pure German-language environment, wasting years on mastering the tedious grammar and vocabularies that have once produced some of the most *weltfremd* (incomprehensible) works of philosophy in the world, leads to nowhere in life today and should...no, must be considered a serious handicap.

Hence the German elites, preaching water but drinking wine, are sending their precious offspring abroad: to schools, summer camps, and universities in the US or UK. And if the parents don't have so much foresight, their kids will have to master English anyway —only later in life, more costly and time consuming, and the harder way.

To prevent the exodus of German education, universities are forced to do two things: First, they have to offer degrees for free (no study fees); Second: they must offer English as the language of academic instruction, even if it were only as shallow as to attract more foreign students who would otherwise pass on Germany and migrate into the Anglophone world. Meanwhile, when Germans venture abroad, walking the streets of Shanghai, Bangkok, or New Delhi, they will always be first and foremost addressed as Americans. Why, because that is what they are: They are "Western people," which, really, is just another polite way of saying they are Accessory Americans.

How could it come to this? Well, if nations have a metaphorical life, there are some which ruined their youth and adulthood; they can't be leaders anymore (while others did just fine). Modern Germany, founded in 1871, is such a troubled nation. It came *late* to the industrialization; *late* to empiricism, *late* to the enlightenment; *late* to democracy; *too late* to libertarianism, individualism, feminism, and *late* to almost all other Western movements, with fatal consequences to its character development and level of maturity.

Germany also was, frankly speaking, a poor imperialist and colonial power: It never got the hang of multiculturalism; despised otherness, and remained racist, conservative, and hierarchic; and the fact that Germany notoriously treated all foreigners with contempt, started both World Wars, and initiated the holocaust, defeated its already radical reputation as a militant people and jeopardized its right to national self-determination forever.

When Anglophone intellectuals think of the German soul, they think of Dr. Faustus who sold his soul to the devil; or Dr. Frankenstein the crazy scientists who created a monster; or the stone-cold, bloody Nazi-man with his Panzer, Blitzkrieg, and bratwurst. Consequently, many German loanwords in English have negative connotations, such as anschluss and gestapo, angst and dreck, flak and Führer.

Thus, whenever the Germans flex their muscles in this 21st Century, their criminal past catches up with them: all those war-crimes, atrocities, the final solution, the holocaust. Without permanent supervision, and letting them known that they are supervised (!), the Germans would immediately fall back on their racist antics, white nationalism, and cultural intolerance. Of course the United States put all Germans under constant surveillance. It's a moral imperative.

During the period of de-Nazification, German history books were revised and approved by US administrators. Tens of thousands of violent newspeak had to be removed and eradicated from the German vernacular, terms like Aryan, Lebensraum, Mischlinge, and judenrein. Patriotism was stomped. At least three generations of Germans, all deemed Nazi, had to be shamed and dishonored –unprecedented in the history of the world. Usually, people are proud of their ancestors, no matter what. Not so the Germans. Despite horrible massacres and crimes against humanity of their own, neither the Americans, nor the British, the Turks, the Slavs, the Arabs, the Persians, not even the Japanese have ever cut off their ancestors or shown similar acts of disloyalty to their fathers and grandfathers so completely and thoroughly as those Germans did. The Germans, seeing an opportunity for dumping their tribe and joining a new one, broke with their civilization, abdicated the Germanic culture, and, naturally, humiliated and broke, readily volunteered for US adoption.

The occupying Western forces (USA, United Kingdom, and France) supervised the German Basic Law, the 'Grundgesetz', in order to ensure liberal democracy, human rights, and capitalism –the latter being a form of warfare without actually killing people. In the intellectual realms, the process of total Westernization was most severe: The hapless Germans witnessed the collapse of all Deutsche Wissenschaften: not only did over one million intellectuals migrate to the United States, taking their disciplines with them, but orphaned German technologies, ideas, and theories were quickly picked up by more resourceful Anglo-Saxon scholars and translated into English. German literature and the academia today are only as good as some Anglophone critic endorses them to be. The remains… the unprocessed German knowledge: a useless crapulence. The Germans lost their 'Deutungshoheit' –the sovereignty over the definition of their own thoughts. Only if US thinkers and authorities discover and acknowledge it does German knowledge exist.

In contrast, the history of the USA was a single coherent success story. Every German kid wanted to be American, because –as school indoctrination ensued- the German past was deemed shameful until, luckily, the Americans came to liberate Europe.

That said, Germans were all still trapped in "being German," were they not, with the consequence that when they grew up, their cognitive predicament developed into a cultural psychosis: nasty emotional swings between two extremes: a massive inferiority complex towards everything American, and an ugly demeanor of superiority toward other cultures. For centuries obsessed with genealogy (bloodline), the Germans are now told by America that a person's deeds and character, not his ancestors, determine his value. From the founding of their nation trained in the art of comformism (hiding in the group), the Germans are now told by America that they have the right to individuality. Like a bastard child raised in a better family with superior values, Germany secretly hates America, but has nowhere near as good to go, and thus picks upon the other, not-so-privileged non-Western kids, telling them they are no good (e. g. patronizing the Muslim world, lecturing the Chinese, belittling the Indians, and hectoring the Russians) –all while hiding in big America's pockets.

Under US global leadership the Germans were allowed to rebuild their Länder with generous US loans but forbidden to centralize its political, economic, and cultural power. Other than Britain with its London, or France with its Paris, Germany remains a republic and federation of 16 states, with 16 governments. Berlin, a city state, and the German capital only on paper, is poor, hippy, and weak in terms of its GDP per capita. And, just like the Soviet Union created former East Germany in its own image, so did the United States a magnificent job in transforming West Germany into a backyard for US capitalists, military deployments, and Europe's greatest outlet for the *American Dream.*

The once so proud Germans, whose ancestors defeated the Romans, repelled the Napoleonic forces, and who once built a German Empire of their own, were now officially *relieved* from the heavy burden of continuing History – History with a capital 'H'. To carve out for them a meaningful existence, they were encouraged to, or driven into, their craftsmanship: assembling automobiles, washing-machines, and words like Elementarfunktionszusammenhänge.

Germany never seriously clashed with America's interest -not even during the Vietnam and Iraq wars which were, after all, modeled after the liberation of Nazi Germany- because the new Federal Republic profited immensely from being the West's cherished prototype of defeat and successful integration into Washington's 'New World Order'. What is more, New Germany has now become the poster child for massive cultural reprogramming efforts in the future, should US administrators ever gain access to the lands and societies of its ideological foes and enemies such as China, Russia, and Iran.

The subjugated Germans are now comet-trailing US imperialism into all corners of the world. It's very profitable, but terms and conditions apply: Berlin has to prostitute itself to Empire. Accordingly, there will be no serious resistance to US mass surveillance on the German people, because that is in the nature of their relation. If there ever was a sovereign and free German spirit, it has long gone kaput.

AN INTERVIEW ON LANGUAGE IMPERIALISM

Chinese Erroneously Translated: German scholar thinks *shengren* are overlooked

BEIJING – The German scholar Dr. Thorsten Pattberg spent eleven years at Edinburgh, Fudan, Harvard, Tokyo, and Peking University to slake his thirst for East-Asian languages and thought. He insists that many Western translations of Chinese key terms are wrong. In this exclusive interview with veteran journalist Victor Fic, he calls for a respectful accuracy and opposing "language imperialism."

Victor Fic: You have an unusual background. Tell us where you were born, and what brought you to China.

Thorsten Pattberg: I was born into a family of police officers in Hamm, Germany. At working-class school I was a notorious underachiever, bored, and playing pen and paper role playing games most of the time. At fifteen, I left school and worked at the Local District Court as a typist. At eighteen, I was transferred to Münster, a university town. There I was encouraged by my superiors to sit the German Abitur. I did it in 2001, and scored well into the top 2% of the entire German student population.

VF: Why did you decide that you must leave Germany if you wanted to learn something new?

TP: The German-speaking world represents a mere 1.2% of the world's population. But if you live long enough in it, they make you think it's 100%. And, German is my mother tongue, so I reasoned that the only way for me to learn something entirely new was to learn other languages in foreign lands.

VF: You first went to Scotland, then China, Japan and the USA to study Sanskrit and Chinese, why?

TP: I actually first went to Oxford University, but was quickly turned down at interview stage. I was told I was too old and too German. Then I looked north and went to Edinburgh instead, where I studied many languages such as Chinese, Sanskrit, Swedish, and later, abroad, Hindi and Urdu. I also spent long summers in

Paris, Tokyo, Boston, Beijing, and Shanghai. But I knew what I was really looking for — to study the sages.

VF: In the west, we prefer philosophers.

TP: That's right. Since Plato's attack on the *sophos* or those who claim to have wisdom, the west embraced a new type of thinker: the *philo-sophos* or those who seek knowledge. There is a big difference between them. The philosophers see wisdom as an unattainable goal and as man's hypocrisy. Maybe Jesus Christ was the last sage, who, in a cunning move before his departure, delegated the highest wisdom to his father in heaven – the Lord God. After the rise of Christianity, the West's sages gradually disappeared. Sage traditions like Confucianism, Buddhism, Taoism, and even Hinduism could never have arisen or caught on in Europe. To use a metaphor: we are immune to them because the Hellenic and Christian tradition runs through our veins. Hence the controversial remark, I think, by Edmund Husserl, a scientist by the way, that "we Europeans, if we understand ourselves properly, would never indianize ourselves, for example."

VF: What is the difference between a Western philosopher and an Oriental sage?

TP: The major difference, I believe, is that a philosopher relies on his sound judgment and argument, while a sage relies on his wisdom from life-experience. About a philosopher, the first thing we want to know is: what is the philosophical object?; about a sage, we want to know: who is he, or what did he do? The sage has to be an exemplifying good person. A philosopher can be a hook and crook, even a Nazi like Martin Heidegger. Everyone can do philosophy, but not every philosopher is a sage.

VF: Why are there so few sages in the west?

TP: Linguistically, there are none. We don't call our thinkers sages. In Germany, the word for sage is "Weiser," but it's *not* a proper title or even a name for any Germany thinker, not even for Goethe or Meister Eckhart. German (and Anglo-Saxon) universities hand out "PhDs" or "doctorates of philosophy." We are, of course, sentimental about what we lack: A good example is how we think of old people in the west as unproductive, undesirable; and we lock them away in nursery homes for the elderly. Yet, they are the ones with life-experience and wisdom.

VF: So such callousness drives Westerners like yourself to search for sages?

TP: I love the symbolism in the award-winning Hollywood blockbuster *No Country for Old Men*, an ultra-violent, shocking tale about a society that has lost its moral compass. According to the Jewish directors, Joel and Ethan Coen, the movie's title and book title, by author Cormac McCarthy, are based on the poem *Sailing to Byzantium* by Irish writer William B. Yeats. If you look it up, you will see that what Mr. Yeats is really mourning about is the absence of sages in the west. That's why his poetic self travels to the east.

VF: Do you argue that the East is a more humane place than Europe?

TP: It is definitely more spiritual, and, in the case of Buddhism or Confucianism, as Gottfried Leibniz in his *Novissima Sinica* and Bertrand Russell in his *The Problem of China* both pointed out, in many ways more advanced in the humanities.

VF: How does this apply to your present home?

TP: China to this day is a living sage culture. It's exactly this expression of humanity that is lacking in the west, at least, if we are honest to ourselves about our limitations, and if we promote a holistic worldview that somehow values *all* human achievement. The West, however, is very different; it believes it lacks nothing: The Western way of thinking is very linear. Western philosophy and Christianity are supposed to be the *single most advanced* cultural mode; all others are seen as deviations from the Western standard. The East is expected to westernize.

VF: Don't Chinese also apply the wrong labels to Western ideas?

TP: Actually, in comparison they usually do not. They keep their socio-cultural originality to themselves. That's not always a good thing – it's too passive. They have too much respect for the West. Chinese students are eagerly studying, and often imitating the West. Same with

Japanese students. But the Western understanding of East Asia is still a murky confusion. Ask a group of Western students, when is the Chinese New Year? What year do we have in Japan? They will most likely think you are an idiot and reply: "Of course, it's the year 2012 AD" –the Year of Our Lord Jesus Christ. The correct answers are: "Long nian" or year of the dragon, Jan 22nd; and "Heisei" or the current emperor's reign 24th year.

VF: Do Western scholars and missionaries ever get it right?

TP: Some of the few archetypes that escaped Western language imperialism are the buddhas and bodhisattvas. Still, Western scholars call Buddhism a religion. This has everything to do with what the Germans call *Deutungshohheit* – the prerogative of the final explanation. Think about concepts like "human rights" or "democracy." The West wants to dominate foreign cultures intellectually; since it cannot *own* Indian, Chinese, or Japanese culture, it still wants to control world history. And it does so by monopolizing names and definitions. Language matters, or, as the Slovenian philosopher Slavoj Zizek once put it: "The ultimate victory (the negation of the negation) is when the enemy speaks your language."

VF: What do Western language imperialists do; they think of Confucianism as a religion or superstition?

TP: The West doesn't have a word for it, so they [the scholars] instead call Confucianism a religion or philosophy or superstition. Confucianism is a 教 *jiao,* a teaching

VF: Who is Confucius in your framework?

TP: Confucius is a 圣人 *shengren.* A shengren is the highest member in the East-Asian family-based value tradition, a wise person that has the highest moral standards, called 德 *de.* He applies the principles of 仁 *ren,* meaning benevolence; 礼 *li,* meaning ritual; 义 *yi,* meaning righterousness; 智 *zhi,* meaning wisdom; and 信 *xin,* meaning faithfulness. There are ten more principles, too. He connects between all the people as if they were, metaphorically speaking, his family. Calling the shengren "philosophers," "saints," or any other familiar name is the greatest historical blunder since Christopher

Columbus's discovery of "the Indians" in America.

VF: Modern Chinese themselves often call Confucius a 哲学家 *zhexuejia*, a philosopher.

TP: Maybe they want to be seen as modern and pro-Western. The word "philosopher" doesn't appear in the Chinese classics. Our so-called "Chinese Philosophy" departments in Europe and America are reminiscences of the imperial past. In fact, the Chinese word for philosophy, 哲学 *zhexue*, came to China via Japan, where it is pronounced *tetsugakusha* ,and was first used in 1874 by Nishi Amane.

VF: What did ancient Chinese correctly call him?

TP: Confucianism talks about five grades: 庸人 *yongren*, 士人 *shiren*, 君子 *junzi*, 贤人 *xianren*, and 圣人 *shengren*. People usually assigned Confucius the highest grade: a shengren.

VF: Are there shengren in China today?

TP: Yes, but this title is bestowed upon them *a posteriori*. The famous writer Lu Xun of the 1930s who explored China's modern dilemma is regarded as a modern shengren. Ji Xianlin is a renowned indologist, writer and educator. He is called a linguist-shengren, and so on.

VF: Are there any scientist-shengren?

TP: Yes, the late Albert Einstein is a scientist-shengren. But, to be sure, we in the west don't have such a classification yet. We need to learn it first. It's a bit like the Western concepts of "artist," "scientist," and "philosopher," that were introduced to first Japan and then China in the late 19th century. If the East now were to return the favor and offer new concepts to us, I mean, why not? It's simple reciprocity.

VF: Is Mao Zedong considered a shengren?

TP: No, Mao distanced himself from Confucianism, and to my knowledge was never referred to as shengren.

VF: How come this alleged language imperialism isn't much known in the West?

TP: It will be as more independent Western scholars learn Chinese and demand adopting Chinese terminologies that accurately reflect the reality of things. As Confucius once said: "If names are not correct, language is not in accordance with the truth of things." It's known as *the rectification of names*. Think about it as cultural property rights. The East invented tens of thousands of non-European concepts we may have never heard of.

VF: How do Chinese or Westerners react to your ideas?

TP: I am ostracized. During my time at Harvard, I tried to present my research at the Fairbank Center, but was banned under the pretext that I was "only a grad student." The German Academic Exchange Service revoked my China full scholarship. In the German community I am outlawed because I studied in China, the ideological enemy of the West. German journalists avoid me like jaundice. Western academic publishers shun my work. But that's ok; the first guy always goes through the wall. Adopting Chinese or any other Asian concepts is threatening the way we do things in the west.

VF: Why do these issues provoke your interest?

TP: I'm just doing my job. I know Chinese. History has been messed up by erroneous Western translations. So now, when I bring on the real stuff like shengren, junzi, daxue, wenming and so on, the public begins to realize: that's a new word, not one of ours…hell, we are not alone! Also, showing respect for another culture's socio-cultural originality goes a long way.

Victor Fic is a writer and broadcaster.

Note: This interview took place in March 2012.

ABOUT THE AUTHOR

Thorsten Pattberg (裴德思 *Pei Desi*) is a German writer, linguist, and cultural critic.

He has written and published extensively about Global language, Competition for terminologies, and the End of translation. He is also active in promoting Confucianism, in particular Chinese terminologies, on a global scale.

He attended Edinburgh University, Fudan University, Tokyo University, and Harvard University, and earned his doctorate degree from The Institute of World Literature at Peking University. He studied under the guiding stars of Ji Xianlin, Gu Zhengkun, and Tu Weiming, whom he considers his spiritual masters.

Dr. Pattberg is currently a Visiting Fellow at the Institute for Advanced Studies on Asia, University of Tokyo; and a former Research Fellow at the Institute for Advanced Humanistic Studies, Peking University. He is the author of four monographs '*The East-West dichotomy*,' '*Shengren*,' '*Holy Confucius*,' and '*Inside*

Peking University,' and some of his representative articles are 'Language hegemony – It's shengren, stupid!,' 'Long into the West's dragon business,' 'China: Lost in Translation,' and 'The end of translation.'